The BluePrint
for
Black Youth Empowerment

THE BLUEPRINT
FOR
BLACK YOUTH EMPOWERMENT

Organizing To Secure Our Future

By Vernon Jackson, ESQ

The Blueprint For Black Youth Empowerment
Vernon Jackson
BPM
www.buildingpowerfulminds.com

Vernon Jackson
"The Blueprint For Black Youth Empowerment"

© 2017, Vernon Jackson
BPM
www.buildingpowerfulminds.com

ALL RIGHTS RESERVED. This book contains material protected under International and Federal Copyright Laws and Treaties. Any unauthorized reprint or use of this material is prohibited. No part of this book may be reproduced or transmitted in any form or by any means, electronic or mechanical, including photocopying, recording, or by any information storage and retrieval system without express written permission from the author.

ISBN 978-0-692-83671-2

TABLE OF CONTENTS

Opening...7

Chapter 1 A Bit of My Background....................9

Chapter 2 Required Attributes........................15

Chapter 3 Steps in Building the Organization...........41

Chapter 4 BPM Strategies and Methods................69

Chapter 5 A Few Keys In Empowering Young Black Males.79

Chapter 6 The BPM Gun Club........................85

Chapter 7 From an Organization to a Movement........89

Chapter 8 Dangerous Wannabes......................93

Closing..99

OPENING

Every Black person on earth has a vital role to play in the economic and political liberation of our people. Those roles are as different, numerous and wide ranging as the problems we face. Each of us must find our role and get to work building and producing for our people in that lane. My role is to organize, fight for and empower black youth, particularly our young Black males. Your role may be entirely different from mine, but regardless of what you determine your role will be, it is necessary to know what skills and methods are necessary in organizing our people and bringing your vision into reality. This book will walk you through how I came to my role, became knowledgeable in my subject area, moved my vision into reality and grew it to, fortunately, have a tremendous impact on in my community.

CHAPTER 1

A BIT OF MY BACKGROUND

I WAS BORN IN Orlando, Florida, in 1986 to Vernon and Sylvia Jackson. I was raised in the roughest parts of the city (Mercy Drive, Ivey Lane, Malibu). My father is an extremely talented man, very intelligent and extremely persuasive, yet he never realized his potential. He battled drug and alcohol addiction and is now a convicted felon. My mother has always been an extremely hard worker with extraordinary faith in Jesus Christ. She has held our family together through very rough times and raised me and my five siblings with the spiritual foundation of Christ. As one of six children raised primarily by a single mother below the poverty line, we experienced multiple stints without lights and water. Although my mother has worked hard every day of her life, we had to utilize food stamps and be creative in making ends meet.

I have had friends killed by the police and friends killed by peers. My oldest sister died of AIDS before I was ten years old. My older brother has greatly influenced my life, however because of our surroundings he became entangled in the criminal justice system very early in his life and could not escape the crippling label that comes with a felony conviction. Growing up, I had a number of family members who were renowned and skilled drug dealers, but very few of my family members had experience in graduating college, gaining profitable skills and accumulating wealth in legal ways. I grew up experiencing all of the things that come to mind when words like "ghetto" "inner city" and "urban lower class" are thrown around. Despite all of this, aside from rare, extreme times of turmoil, I loved every second of my childhood.

Despite the hardships I encountered, my life was centered and well organized around three major points, God, sports and school. I took the spiritual training that my mother provided for me and my siblings very seriously. I worked hard to live the principles that I was taught and not just allow them to "go in one ear and out the other." Early in life I realized that I possessed an intense love for the game of football and any other sport requiring strength, toughness and determination. I also realized that I hated the system that left so many Black people impoverished, unemployed and the main targets of police brutality and mass incarceration. I remember my mother being stopped by the police as she walked home from the meat store. The

A Bit of My Background

police flat out told her that she was the suspect in a recent robbery and that she needed to go ahead and admit to the crime. All of their accusations were 100 percent false. I was not with her during this confrontation but such police harassment and oppression in my community was common throughout my childhood.

My love for and commitment to football took me very far. I earned a full scholarship to the University of Iowa. I graduated from Iowa with honors in Political Science before heading to law school. I graduated from Florida Coastal School of Law with honors and passed the Florida Bar Examination on my first attempt. I have worked for myself since graduating from law school, building my own successful criminal defense practice. Throughout my years in college and law school and as a practicing attorney, I have always been focused on impacting the lives of young Black males who face the same obstacles I faced growing up.

I stumbled into the world of youth empowerment as a sophomore at the University of Iowa sometime between 2006 and 2007. During that time there was a major influx of Black people from Chicago to Iowa City because of the escalating gentrification in the "Windy City." While the newcomers looked and acted in ways that were common in my childhood neighborhoods, many Iowa City residents were not prepared to deal with "those types of Black people." I would often hear snide and condescending comments from Whites and even Black Iowans around the Iowa campus about Black Chicagoans. It was not long before the Iowa City police and other city authorities began instituting various measures to keep an eye on and control these new groups of Black Chicagoan teens that often congregated near the University and often wore hoodies and other "urban" garb.

Although I would often see these youth while I was walking around campus, I did not initially approach them, not because of a lack of interest or concern but because where I grew up being "too friendly" was considered a very negative trait. However, after walking past these young people a few times I was moved to greet them and open lines of communication. I began to understand even deeper that the people on campus who looked at these Black Chicago youth with suspicion and fear, also looked at me the exact same way despite my educational attainment and relative celebrity as a college football player. This external feeling of opposition, animus, and isolation strongly bonded me with these young people.

One day as I walked home from class, I spotted a group of Chicago youth hanging near the Old Capitol Mall, which was located near the center of the University and was a popular lunch gathering and hangout spot for the college students and city residents. I approached a young man in the group named Milton and struck up a conversation with him. The young brother was about fifteen years old and he and his family had only very recently moved to Iowa City from Chicago. From that point on that young brother became like a son to me (although I was just 21 or 22 years old at the time). My friends used to jokingly ask me where I found the young man and would always say "here comes Vern and his son" whenever they saw us together.

That relationship lead me to an organization called "The Spot," which was ran by a young prodigious man named Doug Fern. Doug was an honest and hard-working local activist who had been assigned by his church to do something to help the wave of newly arriving Black Chicago youth. Doug was white as was the overwhelming majority of his church. However, Doug was conscious and humble enough to realize and accept that there were some things that he would never be able to teach Black kids because he could not fully relate to them. Nonetheless, Doug still managed to build a good rapport with a lot of the Black youth and was having some real successes with them. Doug recruited me to "The Spot" as a "positive black male role model." I was and remained extremely humbled and grateful for that opportunity and from that day forward not a day has gone by where I was not strategizing, planning, studying and organizing ways to impact Black youth and destroy the school-to-prison pipeline. That work is God's mission for my life and it has been my undying passion for the past ten years. This passion is what eventually led me to create The Building Powerful Minds Youth Empowerment Program (BPM).

This book is not an autobiography, but I have included a brief summary of my life simply to demonstrate the specific experiences that have allowed me to identify with Black youth who are confronting similar hardships and motivate and inspire them to overcome them. Because of the enormous impact BPM is having in the lives of Black youth around the country and the enthusiastic feedback I have received from people seeking to implement the BPM formula, I decided to lay out in book format all the steps and strategies we utilized in building BPM. It is my hope that the information contained in this book will aid in our efforts to empower our youth, organize our communities and secure a future of our people.

CHAPTER 2

REQUIRED ATTRIBUTES

BEFORE ONE MAKES the costly and taxing, yet rewarding and exciting decision to dive into the battlefield of advocating for, teaching, and empowering young Black males, I believe there are certain core qualities that one must possess. These are the qualities I have depended on the most in my ten years of working to elevate the spirits and minds of our Black male youth. These qualities are essential for any person seeking to make a long term positive impact in the lives of these youth for a number of reasons. First and foremost is many of our Black male youth are severely emotionally and psychologically traumatized and so anyone seeking to reach them must have enough spiritual, mental and emotional strength to remain in a long hard fight while simultaneously lending strength and energy to torn and hurting youth.

The following is a list of the crucial attributes that one seeking to build in this area must possess.

Attribute (1): Acknowledgment and Understanding That Young Black Males Are Under Attack in America

From the onset of the Trans-Atlantic Slave Trade, throughout hundreds of years of chattel slavery, followed by the institution of the convict lease system, Jim Crow and mass lynching, the "War on Drugs," and police and vigilante killings (such as the murder of Trayvon Martin) young Black males in America have always been and still are the targets of intense spiritual, intellectual, psychological and physical violence, subjugation and destruction. Today young Black males stand at the center of a perfect storm of racist and capitalist interests which profit from their miseducation, overmedication, mass incarceration, and economic castration. The underfunding of urban public schools based primarily upon property taxes, the profit-driven push to medicate Black boys for normal juvenile and adolescent behavior, the sick and violent music that is pushed upon them, the genetically modified and poisonous cheap "food" that is prevalent in their neighborhoods, and a criminal justice system that is hostile toward Black males and does more harm than good to them all work to keep our young Black males ignorant, confused, poor, marginalized and non-competitive. Anyone seeking to empower our youth must acknowledge and understand these facts.

Specific Methods of Attacking and Destroying Our Young Males

Miseducation

"It was well understood that if by the teaching of history the white man could be further assured of his superiority and the Negro could be made to feel that he had always been a failure and that the subjection of his will to some other race is necessary the freedman, then, would still be a slave. If you can control a man's thinking you do not have to worry about his action. When you determine what a man shall think you do not have to concern yourself about what he will do. If you make a man feel that he is inferior, you do not have to compel him to accept an inferior status, for he will seek it himself. If you make a man think that he is justly an outcast, you do not have to order him to the back door. He will go without being told; and if there is no back door, his very nature will demand one."-Carter G. Woodson

The vast majority of American public schools miseducate our young black males through Eurocentric curricula that conveniently leave out ancient Afrikans' vast and impressive history of achievement of (from Timbuktu to Kush and Kemet). This purposeful marginalization or erasure of Afrikan history and achievement indirectly tells young Black males that they come from a people who have no history of achievement. Such messages conveyed through inadequate, Eurocentric curricula insult and degrade our youth while killing their confidence and injecting them with a sense of inferiority.[1] Due to the marginalization and erasure of Afrikan history our young Black males are deprived of information that would motivate and inspire them. Dr. Carter G. Woodson wrote so eloquently about this issue decades ago in is classic work, "The Mis-Education of The Negro," yet years later the curricula in the vast majority of American public schools brush over or wholly exclude any substantive study of Afrikan and African American history (aside from the month of February) as well as any real analysis of the historical socioeconomic and racial obstacles that Black people have had to contend with since the inception of this nation.[2]

In addition, under the US approach to funding public schools and current Supreme Court precedent, it is perfectly legal and acceptable that in many affluent areas the amount of money invested in educating each public school student can be (and often is) more than double the amount invested in the education of public school students in economically depressed areas.[3] Under this system our boys attend schools where the teachers are often overworked, underpaid and on top of that bound to a Eurocentric curriculum that does not interest our youth. Afrikan/Black history and the connections of that history to the present are not taught in any meaningful way in the public school system and the deleterious psychological impact this has

---
[1] The Mis-Education of The Negro, Carter G. Woodson, 1933, pg7-8, 19- 22, 68-70, 107-108.
[2] Multicultural Education: Issues and Perspectives, James A. Banks, pg 234.
[3] San Antonio Ind School District v. Rodriguez, 411 U.S. 1.

on our youth is real and major. Without this knowledge our youth cannot form an accurate and positive sense of identity, they cannot understand the scope and nature of the societal forces they encounter, and cannot fully grasp the need for education and the proper way to utilize education to improve their actual lives.

The Criminal Injustice System

As a practicing criminal defense attorney I can say, without a doubt, the criminal justice system is this country's most blatant and vulgar expression of overt anti-Black animus. America's anti-Black system of laws, rules, regulations and penalties is the leading force in the destruction of young Black males. The powers that be (schools, local/state governments, the federal government, wealthy corporations, etc) plan for and track our young males into the prison system from an early age.[4] The treatment young Black males receive at every phase of the criminal justice system is negatively impacted by the color of their skin. Although studies have shown that Black and white youth use drugs at similar rates, with any variance often showing higher usage for white youth, Black youth are much more likely to be stopped, arrested, formally charged, charged as adults and incarcerated.[5] Prosecutors routinely target Blacks for harsher penalties

---

[4] Criminalizing Education, Nancy A. Heitzeg, Ph.D., https://www.hamline.edu/uploadedFiles/Hamline_WWW/HSE/Documents/criminalizing-education-zero-tolerance-police.pdf.
[5] The New Jim Crow, Michelle Alexander, 2011, pg 99, 118.

than they do whites throughout the various stages of the pre-trial negotiation process.[6]

The policing system began in the United States as slave patrols because slave owners and their allies' desired to surveil, control, secure, and contain enslaved Africans. Slavery evolved into the convict lease system which later evolved into the Jim Crow system. The Jim Crow system evolved into the "War on Drugs" and mass Incarceration.[7] Whatever the name, the main aim and impact of these systems have been to criminalize, control and marginalize Black males. As it was then, it is now.

Drugging Our Boys To Death

"The system will take a black man and incarcerate him for years for selling crack and then turn around and pump his son full of the same drug in prescription form for misbehaving in school." -Dr. Umar Johnson

A modern prong in the attack on our youth is the profit-driven strategy of schools and large pharmaceutical companies to arbitrarily label our youth with one or more learning/behavioral disabilities, place them on an alternative educational track and then push unproven, powerful, psychotropic medications to the child's parents as the solution. The sad truth is that in schools around the country those that profit from brain dead, economically castrated young Black men (private prisons and pharmaceutical companies) are getting

---

6 Id. at 117
7 Id. at 20-58

Required Attributes

a head start at sealing the fate of our boys by having them arbitrarily diagnosed with subjective unprovable learning disabilities and then pumping them full of harmful mind-numbing drugs.[8]

I have been told on multiple occasions by public school staff in Jacksonville, Florida, that certain BPM youth were simply unable to control themselves without these mind altering drugs. I immediately knew those assertions to be untrue because I had personally watched these same youth sit, focus, listen, take notes, and socialize with other children for hours and hours during our BPM sessions WITHOUT ANY MEDICATIONS! If a child is simply incapable of behaving he cannot choose when and where to misbehave and that being the case their ability and choice to behave under the oversight of our BPM staff is direct proof that for the vast majority of them, mind altering drugs are not needed. The impact that these drugs have on our youth is devastating and scary. My wife is a public school teacher in Jacksonville, Florida. She has made it a point to work in schools that serve the most economically depressed neighborhoods in Duval County. She often tells me about young Black males who are given these drugs and turned basically into docile zombies. She has also observed the strong withdrawal symptoms these youth experience when they miss a dosage of these drugs.

What are the future prospects for a young Black male who is put into a slow learning educational track early in

---

8 Psycho-Academic Holocaust, Dr. Umar Johnson, 2013, Prince of Pan-Afrikanism Publishing, pgs 3-9.

life, placed on a drug regimen that alters his mind and given those drugs for so long that his body and mind can no longer function without them?

The Emasculinization of Our Boys and Its Impact on The Black Family

The all-out attack on young Black males that I have outlined has been devastating to the ability and means of Blacks in America to build and maintain strong, cohesive, prosperous family units. It is my belief that this impact and outcome has been intentional. Of all the problems that our brave ancestors faced (overt white supremacy, racial violence, Jim Crow, etc) they were able to take those problems on armed with the foundation and security that comes with having strong family units. Despite overt white supremacy and racial terrorism, in the 1960's and into the 1970's over 75% of Black children were born into married families. Today over 60 percent of Black children are born out of wedlock.[9] It has been well documented that Black children growing up in single parent households are much more likely to live in poverty and face a whole host of other hardships. The decline of the Black family unit arose hand in hand with the deterioration of conditions in many urban areas, the outsourcing of blue collar jobs, the introduction of crack cocaine in our neighborhoods and Ronald Reagan's declaration of a "war on drugs," which was really just a war on urban Black communities.

---

9 Births: Preliminary Data for 2005, The National Center for Health Statistics, http://www.washingtontimes.com/news/2006/dec/1/20061201-084845-1917r/.

Required Attributes

Today the Black community faces new profound and complex issues of a nature that Marcus Garvey, Malcolm X and Fred Hampton may have never imagined. Not only is the American sociopolitical system built to destroy young Black males, it has further perfected a wide range of tactics to turn Black men and women against one another. One of these tactics has been an insidious campaign to influence our young men to believe that they are not obligated to actually be men by any traditional Afrikan/Black definition. If our boys are free to become women then what use do they have for Black women? The imagery that is pushed on our young men in the media coupled with the blatant hostility against traditional gender roles existing in many social and political circles and even the chemicals put into the food our children eat are effectively influencing our boys to believe they should view their gender as "fluid." Instead of striving to find, love, marry, and protect a Black woman, our boys now have the option to BECOME BLACK WOMEN.

The idea that there are anti-Black forces and institutions within America that would want to manipulate the images and food that our young men consume in ways that will decrease their desire to become masculine men (husbands and fathers) and their actual ability to do so, seems controversial and outlandish until you look at the facts. The forces and tactics being implemented to exterminate Black masculinity/strong Black manhood are multifaceted, well organized, and very effective. I will list some of them here:

Chemical Warfare

(A) Atrazine: The most commonly used pesticide in America. This chemical is sprayed onto the vast majority of the fruits and vegetables we eat and it is the most commonly found contaminant in ground and surface water. Studies on frogs, fish and rodents have shown atrazine to turn male animals completely into females to the extent that they can reproduce with other males. Scientists have observed lower testosterone and sperm count in human males exposed to this chemical as well as infertility in women overexposed to this chemical. There are other less harmful compounds that can be used to protect crops, yet this harmful chemical that destroys the biological components of masculinity remains the most widely used pesticide.

(B) Bisphenol-A (BPA): This chemical is used in almost all plastic containers and cans that store our food and water. It frequently leaks into our foods and thus is commonly ingested by us. This chemical acts as estrogen in the male body decreasing testosterone, lowering sperm counts, and increasing sexual dysfunction.

(C) Soy: Soy has been approved by the Federal Drug Administration (FDA) and marketed heavily throughout this country as healthy and beneficial to ingest. Less attention has been given to the numerous scientific studies that have found that soy acts in exactly the same way and has the same effect on males as estrogen. Its effects include hormonal dysfunction, enlarged breast, and decreased testosterone (overall emasculation).[10]

Recent Attacks Via Government Policy

In the spring of 2016, President Barack Obama issued a directive ordering all schools receiving federal dollars to allow students to use the restroom NOT BASED ON THE GENDER THEY WERE BORN, but on whatever gender the child identifies with at the time. Schools that refuse to allow this gender fluidity will lose government funding.[11]

Psychological Attacks

(A) **Fashion:** The powers that be are heavily funding and pushing the promotion of males blurring gender lines in fashion and they are using Black males as the face of this movement. For this reason, Jaden Smith (son of actors Will and Jada Smith) was made the "face of Louis Vuitton's 2016 summer and spring **WOMEN'S** clothing line." So-called Rapper, Young Thug, has declared that he is neither male nor female but a "third gender." He was rewarded with the opportunity to model women's clothing for Calvin Klein. Sean "Puff Daddy" Combs, Kanye West, and a host of other Black rappers have worn dresses publicly.

(B) **Media Images-Indoctrination:** The US media has become oversaturated with images of Black men who are

---

[10] Environmental Signs Suggest Atrazine Is Becoming a Serious Health Threat October 19, 2016, http://articles.mercola.com/sites/articles/archive/2016/10/19/atrazine-health-effects.aspx.

[11] Feds Issue Guidance on Transgender Access to School Bathrooms, May 14, 2016, http://www.cnn.com/2016/05/12/politics/transgender-bathrooms-obama-administration/

totally devoid of any traditional marker of masculinity and easily mistaken for natural females. Shows like "The Prancing Elite" glorify and promote Black males who completely abandon every notion of manhood and take on every possible characteristic of femininity.

Attacks on Our Institutions

Black sororities have faced lawsuits and litigation due to organizations composed of emasculated Black males who claim a sorority's choice to admit only women is a form of illegal discrimination. The fact that we have so many large organized groups of young Black men who so badly desire to be women and join women organizations should serve as a red flag that there are some major issues that we as a people must address.[12]

A crucial part of empowering Black male youth is affirming and confirming for them that they are in fact males and that they should aspire to become strong Black men. If we recede from that simple notion (that young black males should become men and fulfill the roles of men) then we take on a complex and confusing variety of unnecessary issues that are not Afrikan in origin and should not be forced upon us. If our boys do not want to become men then the Black family is doomed.

If your aim is to build young Black males into strong Black men, then it is essential that you have a clear definition

---

[12] Alpha Kappa Alpha Sorority Sued By MiAKA For Discrimination, 6/19/12, http://www.huffingtonpost.com/2012/06/19/aka-sorority-lawsuit_n_1609132.html

of what Black manhood is. In BPM we get our definition of manhood from the traditions and practices of our Afrikan ancestors who have always had a clear understanding of the basic and valuable distinctions that exist between the masculine and feminine principles. This masculine-feminine balance can be seen in the earliest spiritual concepts developed and embraced by our ancestors which always portrayed the masculine and feminine principles as distinct components in a balance that is vital for our survival. The spiritual stories of Ausar and Auset, Nut and Geb, and Isis and Osiris all illustrate this understanding. There are distinct and crucial roles that men and women are naturally equipped to play in maintaining this balance, and the blurring of those roles will bring us as a people no good.

The BPM Definition of Black Manhood: The decision of a black male to willingly take on the mandates of Afrikan manhood. These mandates include the obligation to seek and know God, and to know himself, to raise a black family and to acquire the knowledge and skills necessary to ensure the safety, longevity and prosperity of his family. To work in the best interest of our people over all.

Attribute (3): Knowledge of and Relationship With God

It will be impossible for any man to make a substantial, lasting, positive impact on the lives of many young Black males unless that man has a real and intimate knowledge of and relationship with God. This is because when one views the objective facts concerning the current condition of young Black males, it is very easy to become depressed, overwhelmed, and feel totally hopeless. For this reason the key and essential attribute that anyone stepping into this arena must have is FAITH. The battle we embark on when stepping up to the plate for young Black males is as daunting and imposing as what young David faced against Goliath or what Muhammad Ali faced against George Foreman.

In addition to the clear need for a huge amount of faith in order to succeed in this field, history teaches us that the most impactful leaders who grabbed the attention of, mended and built strong Black males, proceeded from a spiritual perspective. Noble Drew Ali, Marcus Garvey, Elijah Muhammad, Malcolm X, Martin Luther King Jr., Louis Farrakhan, and even prominent leaders of Black street organizations such as Jeff Fort, all were able to connect with and galvanize young Black males by utilizing spiritual appeals and messages. This should come as no surprise due to the fact that Afrikans have always been highly spiritual people who held a high degree of reverence for The Most High and who organized their societies and personal lives based upon those beliefs. It is well documented that even before the Afrikans of ancient Kemet built astonishing megaliths motivated by their belief in The Most High and eternal life, the Afrikans of ancient Ethiopia developed the world's first organized spiritual systems.[13] Even today African Americans outpace all other groups when it comes to a belief in God and adherence to spiritual traditions.[14]

---

13 The Wonderful Ethiopians of the Ancient Cushite Empire, Drussila Dunjee Houston,1926, pg 12.
14 A Religious Portrait of African-Americans, Pew Research Center 1/30/09, http://www.pewforum.org/2009/01/30/a-religious-portrait-of-african-americans/.

Required Attributes

It will also be important in seeking to impact Black youth that the issue of spirituality/religion be approached from and taught in a way that addresses race and class head on, to the extent that the race/ethnicity of foundational religious figures is dealt with in detail. Simply put, the vast majority of Black people in America (including myself) ascribe to some variant of the Christian belief system, but it is unquestionable that Black youth are harmed in serious ways by whitewashed distortions and versions of Christianity AND that these distortions, omissions, and the avoidance of the issue of race all together have caused many Black youth to become angry, resentful, and hostile toward religion. Few Black churches teach that all of the major figures in Judeo-Christian history were Black (from Moses to Christ and St. Augustine). Christ is often described in our churches as a calm, docile, loving, liberal white man who came along and saved everyone without addressing any economic, political or racial issues. Rarely is Christ taught accurately as a revolutionary figure who ALWAYS sided with and stood up for the oppressed as Dr. James H. Cone does in his book, "Black Theology and Black Power."

For these reasons, anyone hoping to make a real connection with and lasting impact on large numbers of young Black males in America, must have a real understanding of and relationship with The Creator as well as the ability to teach and speak on spirituality in a way that addresses racial issues and other important issues pertaining to our youth. As a dedicated and enthusiastic follower of Christ who can point to numerous spiritual, mental, and physical manifestations of the impact Christ has had in my life I always address my youth from that point of view, which is infused with a broader understanding of the Afrikan origins of all three of the Abrahamic religions (Judaism, Christianity and Islam).[15] That said, I do not believe one has to be Christian to impact our youth, but I know any person stepping into this arena MUST KNOW GOD.

Attribute (4): A Leader Must Understand Our History:

"Without a broad understanding of history you cannot ask the right questions about our current condition and when you ask the wrong questions you always get the wrong answers."

Just as a good doctor must know the medical history of his patients, so must anyone seeking to mend and rebuild Black youth know the history of the people that he or she seeks to help. While a Ph.D is not required, an intense and in-depth study of ancient Afrikan history and achievement, the impact of foreign incursions into Afrika, Arab and European enslavement of Afrikans, the colonization and neo-colonization of Afrika, the impact of US plantation slavery on our people, the role assigned to Blacks in the US economic order (past and present) mass incarceration, and racial fear/hostility toward young Black males and other related topics are essential for any Black male youth "physician" to know.

I will attempt to explain the importance of this knowledge

---

[15] African Origin Of The Major "Western Religions", Dr. Yosef Ben-Jochannan, 1970, pgs 55-71.

using a short and simple example. If one were to view a five-minute news broadcast from any major city in 2017 (Baltimore, Chicago, New Orleans, Miami, Memphis, for example) a constant bombardment of poverty, violence and crime mostly involving young Black males is likely to be delivered. With those images flowing through one's head, an easy, almost automatic, reaction would be to ask "what is wrong with these people?" That is a very dangerous question because it assumes an inherent flaw in Black youth has placed them in these conditions. Although many racists, eugenicists, white nationalists, and right-wingers openly ascribe to and espouse such views and beliefs, that narrative is a purposefully created falsity. Anyone with a basic understanding of Afrikan history will know that Black people built the most advanced and well-ordered societies on Earth in ancient times, societies where philosophy, math and science originated and where violence and crime were scorned.[16] In light of that knowledge the question then becomes, "what on Earth has been done to this group to cause them to fall from such great heights and how can those forces be countered?" Those two questions and the inquiries that spring from them are VASTLY different.

A solid understanding of Afrikan and African American history is vital because the struggle you embark upon when entering this field is not new. Why waste time learning from trial and error due to a lack of historical knowledge

---

[16] The African Origin Of Civilization, Cheikh Anta Diop, 1974, pgs 230-233.

when you can study and learn from the successes and failures of our ancestors who struggled on this battlefield before us? Surely Marcus Garvey left some valuable guidelines and principles for us to pick up and advance, but how can we do so if we do not study and understand him and the history associated with his efforts?

Lastly, but certainly not least, anyone hoping to empower young Black males must know and understand history because that is one of the main topics that must be taught to our young Black males. In order to empower our youth we must give them a keen **knowledge of self**, which I define as knowledge of all that composes us as Black males; this includes knowledge of God, our Afrikan ancestors and their accomplishments/failures, and knowledge of our current economic, political and social condition, and how we got into this condition. Without this knowledge young Black males cannot accurately interpret contemporary events and the forces they face. For these reasons anyone one hoping to mend and build our young people must have a requisite level of Black historical knowledge.

Attribute (5): The Warrior Pit bull Mentality:

Pit bulls were originally bred in Europe to be successful in animal blood sports such as bull baiting, bear baiting, and later dogfighting. Because of the grueling tasks these dogs were bred for they had to possess abundant levels of toughness, resilience, the ability to endure pain, and a disposition to actually enjoy being thrown into a dangerous fight. Any man seeking to galvanize young Black males must possess the qualities warrior pit bulls possess. This is not hyperbole, it is a proven fact. I have observed the demands placed upon a person who is successful in this arena. I will outline some of the specific reasons the warrior pit bull mentality is essential in empowering young Black males.

This Mission is Hard:

It is important for anyone stepping into this arena to understand that the odds are against you having very much success. By the age of 14 many of our youth have experienced so much trauma and negative indoctrination that it is extremely hard for anyone aside from God to recapture their minds. The music our youth love is often poisonous to their minds and corrosive to their willingness and ability to receive knowledge. The media does not promote gaining knowledge of self and thinking long-term as "cool." Our youth are being taught a "you only live once, just have fun" – "YOLO" ideology every time they turn on the TV or radio. Many of our youth come from families where multiple generations of the men have been snatched away due to the "War on Drugs." These youth have not experienced very much (if any) strong, positive Black male leadership at all in their lives, and many of them will initially lash out and rebel against such an influence. For this reason, in order to have success you must withstand that initial backlash and be strong enough to tear down the mental and emotional walls inhibiting the growth of our youth.

Wayward Parents:

Another reason that you must have a warrior pit bull mentality is the lack of understanding and support that you will receive from some of the parents you will encounter, EVEN WHEN YOU ARE GOING ALL OUT TO BENEFIT THEIR CHILDREN! Many of the parents raising young Black males simply do not understand there is a war being waged against their sons and that as parents they must do everything in their power to save, protect and prepare their sons. Many of these parents do not understand that the schools their sons attend are subpar, that the prison industry is betting on their sons failing and are actively preparing cells for when they do, OR THAT SPORTS WILL NOT SAVE THEIR BOYS. Many of these parents do not understand the historic, economic, political and racial forces seeking to destroy all young Black males. Because these parents lack this understanding they do not fully appreciate or support those who are willing to sacrifice their time, energy and money to combat the forces seeking to destroy their children.

In my experience building BPM into a national model for impacting Black youth, I have had to deal with some of the most backward thinking, clueless, counterproductive and all around negative "parents" on Earth. We set the program up in a way that provided transportation to and from meetings for our initial group members so all the parents would have to do is have the kids home and ready to go. We would call the night before the meetings to remind the parents to have the boys at home the next morning and the parents would assure us that they would do so. Our staff would show up to pick the young men up ONLY TO BE TOLD "oh, he went to his cousin's house" or "oh, I don't know where he went." We have had parents come to the door drunk, high, and nearly naked when we have arrived to pick up their boys. We have had parents ignore all of our begging and pleading to remove their sons from all sports teams until their grades improved. Those parents would allow their children to continue to play sports even with three or four F's on their report cards.

We have had parents sign their kids up for BPM though they really had no interest in increasing the chances of their child's success and were really searching for a potential boyfriend for themselves. We have had parents come to us begging to help remedy behavior problems in their sons only to become angry with us for punishing them. We have even had parents who teach their sons how to steal from stores, take their kids to the stores, steal along with the kids, and then lie to us in hopes that we could get them and the children out of trouble when they are caught.

We also have experienced some very dedicated, sincere, and hardworking parents who do all they can for their sons and for BPM. They donate, they volunteer, they back our staff up and cheer us on. I only describe the negative types of parents to make it crystal clear to anyone thinking of stepping into this arena that it will not be all "peaches and cream" and thus you must have a warrior pit bull mentality. These boys do not change overnight, nor do their parents, and neither will the condition of our people. Anyone wanting to be a soldier in this fight had better be prepared for an intense and protracted struggle.

Attribute (6): The Leader Must Understand Manhood

It is vital for a man seeking to empower our youth to display a sense of strength, toughness, fearlessness and realness. In Afrikan spirituality and culture there has always been a reverence and observance of the dichotomy and power of the masculine and feminine balance. Simply put, there is a certain way that a man should carry himself and a certain way that a woman should carry herself. In my ten years working with young Black males I have noticed they strongly identify with clear expressions of powerful Black masculinity. To illustrate the point that I am trying to get across I will use a few examples.

I have spoken to various Black male groups ranging from football teams to church youth groups to other mentoring programs. During those speaking events I noticed that although I came prepared with tons of information and statistics I felt would impact the boys and prepare them for the future, due to my stature at six feet and 275 pounds, invariably the main thing the boys initially wanted to talk about was my past football career and the amount I could bench press! Initially I would try to move beyond those topics to what I knew were more important issues but I soon discovered that discussing bench pressing, cage fighting and other tough, grueling physical contests I had been involved in, caught their attention, drew them in, and made them more receptive to all my presentation. Our Black boys have a natural desire to be tough, masculine, strong and fearless and they look for those attributes in their role models.

This fact can be either positive or negative. If our boys can interact with and look up to God-fearing, intelligent, principled Black men who display attributes of toughness, strength and fearlessness, those boys will gain a realistic and balanced idea of what it means to be a "real Black man." On the other hand, if the only strong, tough, masculine Black men our boys see are rappers, drug dealers and pimps, they will get an inaccurate, harmful idea of what it means to be a real Black man.

Another reason it is vital for a man in this arena to display attributes of masculinity, strength and toughness is because Black youth stand in absolute awe when they encounter real authentic expressions of Black masculine strength. I came to realize this in my work with BPM, but even more so in my speaking events at public schools. As I mentioned earlier, my wife is an accomplished elementary school teacher. She demands respect and runs her classroom in a very disciplined manner. On various occasions I would visit her classroom and other classes to speak with and help motivate students. In almost every single classroom I entered, the students (boys and girls) would stop whatever they were doing, come to full attention as if I were an army commander and begin to whisper to each other. This always made it very easy for me to speak to and teach these children, because although they did not know me, they were captivated by whatever I had to say.

Those occasions made me realize the psychological reasons that a kid who has a good father will so quickly say in times of trouble "I'm gonna tell my daddy on you!" Our youth long for and appreciate the security and surety that comes with having a strong, powerful, Black man around who will love and protect them. When they do not have such a figure at home they are even more receptive to anyone who displays the attributes of masculinity, strength and toughness. Again, that fact can be either positive or negative depending on who it is that our kids are looking to for those traits.

Black Youth Can Sense Weakness

In discussing Black youth, my wife and I would often come to the conclusion that "kids know which tree to climb." When in the presence of any adult, Black youth seem to automatically be able to sense whether or not that adult's aura and energy demand respect and obedience or invite disrespect and contempt. Weak, timid, unsure adults are easily detected by our youth and they will gladly and freely "walk all over" those adults. If you aim to impact Black male youth, they must respect you. In order for them to respect you, your attitude and the way you carry yourself must demand respect. If you observe pit bulls of today you will understand they carry the blood of the warrior pit bulls of the past, you will also notice that even in the presence of much larger and more imposing animals, they still walk with no fear or hesitation. They never tuck their tails, they never back down, and they do not even seem to comprehend fear. When dealing with inner city Black male youth, you must carry yourself in the same way. No child wants to follow a weak leader and no child will respect a weak leader.

Attribute (7): Sincerity

I cannot stress enough the absolute vital nature of sincerity of motives in this field of work. A person cannot and will not succeed in truly impacting our youth if that person has hidden, impure, or ulterior motives. I am so certain this is the case because it takes so much time, effort, energy, and money to stay on this battlefield for the long haul that anyone with false motives will soon become disinterested, tired or dejected and will fizzle out. When you are in this fight for the right reasons the youth themselves will empower and rejuvenate you every time you meet. Seeing them wake up, head in the right direction, and take real steps toward true manhood will be all the thanks and glory you need. God will continually bless your spirit and your works will bear fruit. However, if you enter this field seeking notoriety, fame, or other vain benefits, those desires will not be enough to sustain you in this rough and taxing line of service.

A leader in this field must be spiritually and intellectually clear and honest as to his true reasons for wanting to be involved in this work. A person with the wrong motives will simply be wasting their time, stressing themselves out, and further harming our youth. That person will very quickly realize empowering black youth is not a shortcut to fame nor is it a glamorous endeavor. This field of work requires major continued sacrifice and that sacrifice quite frequently occurs with no fan fair and not even a thank you. BE SINCERE.

CHAPTER 3

STEPS IN BUILDING THE ORGANIZATION

Few Clear Goals

It has been proven that organizations or businesses with too many disparate and widespread aims often end up treading water and accomplishing none of their many goals. When I started BPM, I had one burning desire in my spirit and one goal in my mind. That goal was to throw a huge monkey wrench into the system of mass incarceration in America and bust a huge hole in the Black male pipeline to prison. My main goal was to destroy that sick system and that formed BPM's main foundational trajectory.

As a child growing up in the roughest parts of inner city Orlando, Florida I witnessed the real life impact of the prison pipeline every day. Many of my friends in middle school would come to class wearing ankle monitors as a consequence of being on house arrest or some other form of probation after run-ins with the law. My mother told me very early on that she would never come down to bail me out of jail because my oldest brother had required her to do that so many times that he had used up all of our chances to mess up. As I noted in the introduction to this book, my father is a convicted felon and I have visited him in prison on multiple occasions. During those trips I was flabbergasted by the spools and spools of barbed wire lining the huge prison gates, the isolated location of the prison, and the racial composition of those behind the prison walls. That racial breakdown was very simple: the warden, guards, and nurses were white and the inmates were mostly Black. Cops, juvenile detention centers, jails and prisons were as much a part of life for me as church, school and football.

At the University of Iowa I decided to major in Political Science which allowed me to take some very interesting courses. One such course was called "Global Insurgency" and it was taught by a very progressive, white female professor, Adrienne Hurley. It was in this class that I was first exposed to the structured way in which racism combined with unfettered pursuit of the profit motive create entities and forces that devastate Black people. In this class I was exposed to facts concerning the enormous explosion of the prison population in California during the 1960s and 1970s under then Governor Ronald Reagan, a trend he later took nationwide as president. In this class I was shocked to see the well calculated and orchestrated political drive that allowed for the rise of mass incarceration, an effort carried out by professionals who popularized terms like "Super Predator" to describe Black youth. In this class I was first exposed to the sad sadistic impact of placing young teenagers (14 and 15 years old) into prisons with fully grown, highly institutionalized, dangerous inmates when these children had committed crimes that had not resulted in death or great bodily harm to anyone.

After taking that course I began my own study of the US economic and prison systems and was floored as fact after fact demonstrated that profit motive and an anti-Black agenda fueled the growth of the US prison population, not actual violent crime rates or crime period. When I discovered that enormous corporations like Corrections Corporation of America and the GEO Group (Wackenhut Corrections Corporation, at the time) were raking in millions and even billions of dollars largely from the incarceration of non-violent Black male offenders, my stomach turned. I was further floored to learn that when these private prisons opened facilities in various states, the state governments would sign contracts with the prisons to GUARANTEE CERTAIN NUMBERS OF INMATES![17] I was disgusted to find out these private prisons spend millions each year on well-connected lobbyists to push for even tougher legislation to ensure even more inmates.[18]

This knowledge played a major role in my decision to

---

17 Report Finds Two-Thirds of Private Prison Contracts Include "Lockup Quotas" July, 2015, Joe Watson, https://www.prisonlegalnews.org/news/2015/jul/31/report-finds-two-thirds-private-prison-contracts-include-lockup-quotas/.
18 Too Good To Be True, Private Prisons in America, The Sentencing Project, 2012, http://sentencingproject.org/wp-content/uploads/2016/01/Too-Good-to-be-True-Private-Prisons-in-America.pdf

attend law school and become a criminal defense attorney. From the day I arrived at Florida Coastal School of Law, my one foundational goal was to learn everything I could about the US Constitution, federal and state criminal law, and the Florida criminal court system so I could personally combat the mass incarceration of young Black males. During my time at Florida Coastal, aside from the required core courses, I chose to take a number of diverse courses which focused on every aspect of the criminal justice system. Some of the most impactful of those courses were Criminal Procedure and Advanced Criminal Procedure, which focused on the constitutional and procedural rights and protections built into the US criminal justice system; Evidence and Forensic Evidence, which focused on what information and materials could be admitted and considered during legal proceedings and the mechanisms used get them admitted; Wrongful Convictions, which focused on numerous cases wherein legal errors and corruption resulted in defendants being wrongfully convicted and incarcerated; and, Juvenile Justice, which focused specifically on the rules and procedures in the juvenile court system (which vary greatly from the adult system).

In addition to those lecture courses, I was privileged to be able to take three different independent study courses which allowed me to research a legal topic of my choosing and write in depth legal papers on those topics. Through these courses I was able to analyze and break down the "War on Drugs" and its impact on our Fourth Amendment protections, the seemingly certain path from our juvenile detention system into our adult prison system, and the incentives and disincentives created by the welfare system. All of this additional reading, researching, thinking and writing only served to cement my certainty that the US economic and criminal justice systems are structured and functioning in a manner that targets, harasses, brutalizes, kills and incarcerates a shockingly disproportionate number of young Black males. It became even clearer to me that the expansion of the system of mass incarceration was almost 100 percent unrelated to crime rates and the actual criminality of young Black males. With this knowledge of how the system worked I set out to build an organization that would snatch young Black males out of the jaws of that machine and equip them with the spiritual foundation, knowledge, mindset and resources that would prepare them to beat the miserable fate this society has planned for them. That has been and always will be the foundational aim of BPM. With one or two clear goals in mind one is better able to research, study, create and implement sophisticated methods toward achieving those goals. It is tough for a single person or small group of people to become experts in a wide variety of different fields simultaneously and so the most efficient way to building an organization is around a few foundational concrete goals.

Develop Practical Methods Toward Your Goals

Once you have settled on a few main concrete goals you must then strategize and develop practical, feasible methods toward achieving those goals. You must be sure that the methods you adopt are methods that can be instituted and adhered to with a high level of consistency. Your methods must be sustainable and well within your means as far as time, money and other resources. Your efforts must also be tailored and targeted toward your desired impact and not simply symbolic. For example, with the goal in mind of increasing children's academic performance, many people make a big deal every year about having huge "back to school events" through which they provide children with school supplies and a great back to school pep talk. These people feel great about their contribution, receive attention and pats on the back, and then move on probably never seeing those children again (until the start of the next school year). Those kids do benefit from the backpacks and pencils, but if they do not have the right mindset regarding education, they will probably throw those pencils away and use that backpack to store things other than books and school supplies. The strategy of these back to school events, if not paired with long term follow up efforts, is mainly a symbolic show of support for education that will have little to no lasting impact on the children.

I started BPM from a room in my mother's small house on the northside of Jacksonville a few minutes away from Edward Waters College. I was a broke college grad getting ready to start law school. I did not have very many connections in the city as I had been raised in Orlando and went to college in Iowa. For a substantial period of time I did not even have a car. With those limitations in place I began teaching my little brother, who was around nine years old at the time, and his best friend (another young black male who was constantly at my mother's house) all of the things I thought they needed to know in order to avoid the fate I knew this society had in store for them. I would lecture them on Black history and we would discuss past giants like Malcolm X, Martin Luther King, Jr., Fred Hampton, and Huey Newton. I would pull up speeches for them to listen to, take them with me to work out or to the barbershop and pretty much everywhere else I went. We would talk openly and honestly about the fact that as young Black males, the system was already planning and aiming to see them dead or in a jail cell. I talked to them about setting goals and working toward them with unyielding focus and dedication. I treated them both like my little brothers and in many ways like sons.

As people in the community continued to see me with these two young boys, always training and teaching them, they would always ask "are those your sons?" I'd always tell them "no," and that I did not have any children. Some could not understand why I would put in so much time and effort with kids who were not biologically my own. Other People just wanted to know if I would help train their sons. More and more Black parents began to ask if I would work with their sons and I quickly became overwhelmed and badly outnumbered.

Start where you are and use what you have

When it comes to empowering youth and building an organization for that purpose, one of the most damaging and counterproductive tendencies I have seen in people is to declare that they have to wait until they have "everything lined up" and every resource desired before they can or will take action. With that mindset one will never get started. Many people start off with the idea that in order to start reaching youth they must have plenty of money, a glamorous building for meetings, a large army of staff, vans to transport kids, tax exempt government status, etc. All of those things are great to have and will help your empowerment efforts to flourish, BUT not a single one of them is NECESSARY to start impacting our youth.

I started BPM the summer before I started law school at a time when I had no job, no special brick and mortar building, no staff, no money and was living with my mother. Despite that I had a burning desire to impact Black youth and destroy the prison pipeline. I could not wait until I had a law degree, a nice job, lots of cash, and a fully functioning staff. I noticed my little brother and his best friend were always hanging around the house looking for something to do. I knew I had some very valuable information they badly needed as young Black males in Duval County and so I began to teach them. I would give the boys lectures about our history and struggle in America and I was a bit shocked at how receptive they were to the information. They were captivated by Black history and always wanted to know more. I continued to teach them and I was also able to connect with them on the one thing that almost every inner city Black male youth loves, ATHLETICS. As a former Division

I athlete, who still maintained a serious physical fitness regimen, these boys saw me as a real life example of a physically dominant and successful athletic role model.

I began to train those two boys in physical fitness and to use those sessions to also instill principles in them. During a tough portion of a workout or physical challenge, I would yell to them "what's hard?" and they would reply "everything is hard." I'd then yell, "what's easy?" and they'd reply "nothing is easy." I would proceed to go down a list of all the great things they wanted in life, a pretty girlfriend, a good career, good grades, etc., and constantly reiterate none of those things would be easily obtained. Those things would all be hard to get and so they had to learn to be cool, calm, and positive while carrying out hard tasks. This small nucleus and the culture we began developing (knowing/learning our history, working out to build strength, toughness and character, and brotherhood) laid the foundation for BPM which now serves hundreds of children in multiple states. Had I waited until things were perfect in my life to get started, I still would not have started BPM. BPM is now seven years old.

You can start impacting your little brothers, cousins, kids in the neighborhood, etc. You can begin to reach them through sports and other avenues that do not include a fully formed empowerment program from the start. Taking a few of them to Subway, listening to what is going on in their lives, and dropping a few jewels of knowledge on them can make a large impact on those youth. Those basic things also help to lay the foundation for a more structured program in the future. Start where you are and use what you have.

Using Your Resources

Although I always knew that the youth empowerment program I was aiming to build would be unique, controversial, and like no other, I still knew there would be some people and institutions in my community that would be willing to support our mission. One such institution was my church. I knew the church did not have a program of the nature of what I was building and that many Black churches, depending on the composition of the leadership board and member body, would have a serious issue with being associated with a "pro-Black" and specifically Black youth empowerment program. I also knew that a church like mine, located in the heart of the inner city where crime and poverty are rampant would have a hard time turning away an organization that was transforming the very youth the church members would otherwise be seeing on the evening news.

I reached out to my bishop and explained to him the BPM mission. He supported it wholeheartedly and my church became our biggest sponsor. Through our partnership with my church we have been able to obtain meeting facilities, classrooms, transportation, and a whole host of other useful resources. Black churches are frequently the only institutions within impoverished Black communities that have resources and are still operated by Black people. While many "conscious Blacks" hate and berate the Black church, Dr. Huey P. Newton instructed us that as real activists seeking to empower our people, it is unwise to war against the institutions in our communities that the masses hold dear. Though those institutions do not always act in the best interests of the Black masses. Dr. Newton taught us it is more profitable in the long run for committed change agents to influence, mold, and utilize those institutions and their resources in ways that benefit the masses.[19]

Whether it be a church, a community center, or a pro-Black business in the community, always be sure to reach out, network and enlist those entities and their resources in your youth empowerment efforts. That said, be careful to NEVER become dependent on those entities for the continued survival and progress or your group/organization. Relationships can sour and some cannot take the heat that comes with being uncompromisingly pro-Black. You never want to be stuck depending on a person or entity that cannot take the heat.

A Few Good Men

As I began empowering my two initial BPM young men other people soon began taking notice. My brother's best friend began bringing his little brothers to learn and workout. People noticed this small group of boys and knew their sons needed what we were doing. Black parents began to continually ask me to mentor their sons. At that point I realized I could not take in every young Black male in

---
19 To Die For The People, Huey P. Newton P.hD., 1972, pg 60.

Duval County, so I started to actively recruit other solid Black men to help me empower these young brothers. I only reached out to men who embodied the principles that I was working to instill in the boys. At my law school, at the barbershop, around the community, I began keeping an eye out for strong, real, family-oriented brothers who had experienced the hardships of growing up in impoverished inner cities and would be serious about impacting these boys. One fact I learned quickly, and that you must grasp as well, is that THERE ARE ONLY A FEW MEN LIKE THAT.

There are plenty of successful Black men walking around and many of them did have to overcome challenging childhoods, BUT people are generally lazy and uncommitted to things that (A) cost them time, money and energy and (B) don't make them money or benefit them in some visible and direct way. Very few people will make a long term, consistent, passionate commitment to an organization out of the pure and simple desire to empower youth and see them succeed. That type of person is rare BUT you only need a few. When you encounter a brother who is willing to make those sacrifices he will work like hell, stick with the organization, sacrifice his time and spend his own money. He will not be looking for a pat on the back or any sort of fame or accolades in return. He will be a soldier. You will be amazed at how much you can accomplish for the youth with just two or three of these soldiers. Do not be overly concerned about finding 20 or 30 willing volunteers. You may not ever reach that number and it does not matter. Focus on finding two or three soldiers, assess what each is best at, develop roles based upon those strengths, and watch your organization flourish.

As your group/organization gains size, structure and visibility you will attract additional soldiers, as well as people who are willing to help but seeking something in return. Always delineate between these two types of people and never depend on a non-solider as if he or she were a soldier. There are useful roles that non-soldiers can play but never make their productivity or performance of any task of such importance that the functioning of your organization is substantially hampered if that person fails to perform. Assign non-soldiers ancillary roles that help the organization progress yet won't "stop the show" if not performed.

At this juncture I'd like to give a special thanks to Attorney Jonathan Ross and Monika Jackson, two of the most committed and consistent soldiers that BPM has ever had

Plan on Abuse, Misuse and Misunderstanding

If you to step into the gritty arena of empowering the most disadvantaged and miseducated youth in America, you are probably going to be dealing with some of the most troubled and challenging parents in America and you will most likely be operating in one of the most economically depressed areas in America. For all of these reasons you must be ready for a number of slights, insults, abuses, and frequent disrespect. Many youth and their parents do not realize or appreciate the sacrifice and commitment it takes to offer your energy, time, money and love to a child that you did not create. Many of the parents you deal with will drive across town to their favorite night clubs, yet claim they are unable to bring their child out to beneficial events and meetings you plan. They will call you in the middle of a work day when the child gets into trouble at school, yet refuse to follow your advice as far as disciplining the child. Many of them will act as if they are entitled to your services although you offer them on a volunteer basis. Worst of all, many of them simply will not comprehend the war that is being waged on young Black males and the vital nature of your efforts in that war. These parents are nonchalant and flat out careless when it comes to getting their sons the help they need.

You will undoubtedly deal with these types of parents in this line of work and a gut reaction is to think to yourself "I'm wasting my time with this kid due to his parent's ignorance, I should just move on." Do not let that be your first reaction. Always go back to your reason and purpose for jumping into this fight and then consider the socio political knowledge you have concerning how our people got into this condition. With those things in mind, remain patient, humble, and calm. Try to educate the parent and slowly get them to understand the vital nature of your mission. Stay dedicated to empowering the child regardless of the pettiness and short-sightedness of the parent. If you have done all of these things over a substantial period of time and the parent still has made no progress (and that has stunted the child's progress) then and only then do you consider moving on from that particular family.

In addition to ungrateful parents, many powerful, well connected people within the Black community will not possess the care you have for your people and will not lift a finger to aid you in your efforts. Some will even actively work against your efforts. As we sought to grow and expand BPM we were denied access to a number of community centers we sought to use for meeting space. We were questioned, lectured, and derided for focusing specifically on Black kids. We have been looked over when it comes to funding and support in favor of more mainstream/commercial organizations although they were not doing a fraction of what we were doing for our youth or having a fraction of the impact that we were having. We have been called "militant" and "separatists" by Black and white people around the country, simply for teaching our Black boys to love, honor and protect the Black woman.

All of this information is included for the simple purpose of destroying any preconceived notions you may have about "stepping in as a hero, changing kids' lives and receiving fame and glory." Those are false expectations in this field. Fame and glory cannot be your aim and insult and dejection are guaranteed. If you are alright with being knocked down and mistreated EVEN WHEN YOU ARE SEEKING TO HELP YOUR PEOPLE then you have the right temperament for this field. If you want appreciation, reciprocity, and gratitude for everything you do, stay home. This is not the right field for you. Throughout all of the mess, turmoil, and hardship, the one thing that you can NEVER DO IS GIVE UP. NEVER. You cannot be a quitter and help Black people. You must view yourself as a doctor working hard to help a very sick patient, a patient who often does not even realize how sick he is. You can not get discouraged and quit half way through the operation. You must have the resolve and determination to keep grinding and stay the course.

Start Small and Build A Culture

As stated above, BPM's initial youth roster consisted of just two young Black males, my younger brother and his best friend. As parents noticed our efforts and began to put their sons into the program, I made it a point to grow the group very slowly. In fact, for around the first six months of the program we intentionally kept the group at around ten or less boys. I did this so that I could thoroughly reeducate, convince, win over, and train the boys we did have so we would have a powerful and persuasive nucleus when we began adding new youth. I approached the small group that we had using a theory or method I developed called the "Light Switch Method." This method simply means that once a young Black male has been exposed to real knowledge of self (God, history, and society), once his eyes are opened to the forces that oppose him in America, once he has had the disastrous blinders of materialism, instant gratification, and individualism torn from his eyes, a light comes on in his mind and that light changes his entire ideology, shapes his decisions and reroutes his entire life.

Once this occurs the need to constantly discipline, correct, and chastise these young men nearly disappears. This is not to say they become perfect or will not make mistakes, but the foundational way they approach life changes for the better and steers them clear of many of the pitfalls in this society. Once you have a small group of boys who have experienced that awakening and have brought into that way of life (culture) they will automatically influence any new youth who are bought into the group. With that approach in mind, we kept our group small and slowly accepted more and more youth until the flood gates broke and our numbers jumped from 10-15 youth to 20, 30, 40, 50 and on up to currently 70 young men in the Duval County Chapter of BPM. We knew we had to build a culture before we grew in numbers. Once God sees diligence, consistency, and realness in your efforts He will send the youth and the workers. Do not be caught up in numbers early on, be focused on building a culture that will impact the numerous youth who will inevitably come if you keep working.

Reverse Peer Pressure

When we hear the term "peer pressure" it brings to mind images of an impressionable teen who is good at heart but gets into some negative activity because his "friends all do it" and think it is "cool." Peer pressure is a very real and powerful force in the lives of our youth, in fact many scholars have reached the conclusion that a child's peer group will have just as much (or more) impact on their behavior as the child's parents. The great part about the BPM formula is that once you have established a culture of discipline, respect, knowledge of self, and a thirst for learning amongst your initial core group, you will benefit greatly from what we call "Reverse Peer Pressure." Just as a young man can be influenced by those within his peer group to make negative decisions, he can certainly be influenced by those within his peer group to make positive decisions.

When a child enters our program he is not only surrounded by dedicated, successful Black men who will push him in the right the direction, he is also surrounded by an entire peer group that has internalized the BPM principles and will accept nothing less from new members. This energy or pull that impacts new BPM recruits may be the most powerful part of our approach. Here is just a small example, veteran BPM youth know they are required to remain quiet, focused, and attentive when an adult is addressing the group. Older BPM members make sure the younger boys follow this rule and quickly intervene to correct new youth who come in and violate that rule. For this reason I rarely have to tell new BPM youth to "sit down and listen when an adult is talking." Reverse peer pressure immediately impacts new youth and eliminates many of those problems.

One of my proudest encounters with reverse peer pressure occurred as I was taking a few BPM youth home after a meeting and an argument broke out amongst them over who would have the highest GPA at the end of the semester. Every child in my car that day was adamant that he would outdo the others a. I was used to hearing young Black males argue and compete over sports, girls, and/or fashion, so it was refreshing to hear these young Black males arguing over academic excellence.

Peer Based Humbling

In BPM we have always valued strength, toughness, courage and the ability of a man to defend himself and his family. For this reason training in boxing, wrestling, and other disciplines have always been a part of our program. As our program grew and we began to accept more youth the physical component of our approach began to play a separate and extremely valuable role.

One of the most glaring and obnoxious attributes of a young male on the path to destruction is arrogance. Many of the most disrespectful and self-destructive young men that we have encountered, entered the program with a pronounced sense of pride and a belief that they were so tough and real no one could stop them. It is absolutely amazing to see how that bravado quickly dissipates into meekness and regret once these young men are thrown into the combat arena and suffer their first real punch to the stomach or powerful takedown. As they pick themselves up and dust themselves off they realize they cannot fake their "gangster" persona in BPM and that they are amongst real men and young brothers who will test them and see just how tough they really are. Many of these young men are accustomed to being in groups who will back them up in times of conflict or being able to resort to guns whenever their manhood is challenged. In BPM they encounter a totally different situation. There are no friends to step in and save them and no guns to reach for. They are required to prove just how tough they really are and many of them get a serious wake up call. Once these young men experience public physical domination, their entire attitude changes and they "magically" become a lot more humble and easier to teach.

This physical humbling that I speak of is nothing but a slightly different form of the discipline and correction that a strong father provides to his son who begins to get "too big for his britches." Unfortunately, when Black fathers are absent many of our young Black males are allowed to grow up with no one to check their bravado and bring them back to reality. As we all know, a young man who begins to become too cocky and "smell himself" must be put back in his place. Pride goeth before a great fall. The BPM approach enables us to physically shock wayward black males out of their sense of arrogance and make them prove how tough they really are.

Keep It Cheap and Spread The Costs

As you embark upon this journey of impacting youth and building a powerful organization toward that end, you will still have your own personal financial responsibilities, bills and obligations. Although sacrifice is mandatory in this field, you don't want to constantly be putting out so much of your own money that your other obligations lack or fall behind. That will only lead to frustration and discouragement. For that reason, unless you are already independently wealthy, which I most definitely was not when I started BPM; ALWAYS SEARCH FOR THE CHEAPEST POSSIBLE METHOD TOWARD ACHIEVING YOUR GOALS. There are many larger, better funded, more commercial youth organizations in America that spend ten times what BPM spends in a year yet don't have a fraction of the true and lasting impact that BPM has. This is so because it is so easy for an organization and its leaders to become focused on events and efforts that garner lots of media and social media attention, that they lose track of events and efforts that truly enlighten and empower their youth.

Here is an example of phenomenon that I speak of. Many youth organizations make a big deal about large, well-publicized and very expensive road trips for college visits. Taking into account travel, hotel and food costs for any substantial number of youth and volunteers, these trips will inevitably cost thousands of dollars. For big commercial organizations that would not be a barrier, but for me building from scratch, that most definitely would be difficult and maybe unwise to do. BUT HERE'S THE GOOD NEWS!! Instead of going all out to raise 5 thousand dollars to spend on one trip, you can set up SAT/ACT prep sessions in your own city, bring in people who are knowledgeable concerning both tests, do an entire series of prep courses and ensure that your boys can actually qualify for college ALL FOR LESS THAN A FIFTH of what you'd spend on the college road trip. The lasting impact of the latter route would almost certainly be greater while the financial costs would be negligible.

Even today, a BPM session with average turnout (50-55 boys & 10-15 girls) does not cost more than $150. This includes getting the youth to our meeting spot, the lecture, academic tutoring, physical training, and food for each child. Considering the fact that those costs are spread between our core group of volunteers (10-12 adults) that amount leaves no one in a jam at home when bills are due. The rule is simple, search for cheaper activities and events and always spread the costs. Impacting our youth does not have to leave you broke.

501 C3 Non-Profit Status

When building an organization to empower youth who drastically need it, the question of seeking government tax exempt status will inevitably arise. There are benefits and drawbacks to becoming a 501 (C)(3). From my experience building BPM from scratch I can say for certain that tax exempt status is not needed or required to build a successful Black youth empowerment program. For the first four to five years of our program's existence we did not have tax exempt status and did not care to seek it. We built our program in a way that it could run smoothly, impact our youth and continue to grow WITHOUT A SINGLE GRANT OR DONATION. We made sure that even if we received no outside funds or contributions, BPM could function fully on the pooled resources of our dedicated core group of volunteers. That source of funding is the most consistent and most certain and a program should be built to be one hundred percent economically self-sufficient.

As our organization grew we began to inquire about the pros and cons of 501 (C)(3) status. Although we never needed it and were growing just fine without it, we did notice that many other local organizations that were doing far less for our youth were raking in tons of grant/donation money because of their tax exempt status. It occurred to me that if any group should have access to large pools of funding it should be groups that are actually putting in targeted, consistent, meaningful work. On the other hand, we were one hundred percent against anything that would restrain or hamper the stances we could take, the statements we make, or the information we teach. BPM has always had a zero tolerance policy concerning "sugar coating" and any other form of buck dancing, conforming, or tip toeing simply for the purpose of receiving outside support or avoiding outside scorn. I was aware that there would be some such rules/restraints imposed upon us if we took on 501 (C)(3) status. Non-profit organizations are barred from all political activity (aside from general non-partisan activity)-any political/partisan efforts members of a non-profit seek to engage in must be done totally separate and apart from the non-profit organization itself and use none of the organization's funds.

Our ultimate decision came to down to this reasoning process; we did not NEED to take on 501 (C)(3) status but we could certainly raise more funds and impact additional kids if we did. Since we knew we could continue to function perfectly well without tax exempt status we decided to become a non-profit, maintain our strong stances/positions, utilize the added fundraising capabilities that flow therefrom, and, if at some point, we were so "strong and Black" that we were stripped of that status, we would go back to what we knew best, functioning on our own and sustaining the organization without the tax exempt status. After about a year as a non-profit I can say that we have stayed true to our beliefs and have not been stripped of our status. The choice though remains up to each group, your aims, and methods.

Cover Your Butt

It was very important for us as a group of private individuals and later as a non-profit organization to utilize the needed documents, permission slips, notifications, and liability forms to protect us as individuals, business owners, and as an organization. There is a lot of physical activity involved in the BPM approach. We travel at times and participate in various events and activities. With those things in mind anyone seeking to have sustained success in this field must realize that we live in a litigious society and that some parents (regardless of how much you've done for their sons) will seek to profit from any busted lip, sprained ankle or other bump or bruise that the child sustains under your program's watch.

Also, never put your entire organization at risk for one child, parent or volunteer. If a child displays violent or inappropriate behavior that is simply too dangerous to the other youth in your group, you may have to simply kick him out. If a parent is always complaining or finding fault with your organization and efforts, that can become a liability risk, and therefore that family may have to be removed from the program. All of your volunteers should be thoroughly vetted to ensure they can safely and legally be engaged in the type of work that your organization will be doing. You cannot let all of your hard work go to waste due to simple failure to adhere to legal requirements and sound operating procedures.

Too Young = Too Much Trouble?

What age group of youth should you work with? Is there an age group that gives our people the best return on our investment? When we started BPM we intended to work with boys between the ages of 10 and 17. We felt that at ten years old the boys would be able to comprehend and take in the things we were teaching and that younger boys would be hard to control and unable to grasp much of what was being taught. As time progressed that whole view changed, partly through learning and partly due to the fact that most of our boys had little brothers and their parents pushed them into the program as well. As I analyzed the array of attacks that are being unleashed upon our youth from the media, destructive medications, and the school to prison pipeline, it became clear to me that the attacks are targeting our boys earlier and earlier in life. Elementary age Black boys are being tested, labeled, drugged, arrested and criminalized in our public schools every day. The cartoons our little ones are watching are filled with harmful subliminal messages and the system is viewing and treating them like adults, not children.

Simply put, the system is seeking to destroy our youth at very young ages so we have to put focused efforts into building, empowering and reeducating our youth early on in their lives. For that reason we decided to openly accept and recruit boys as young as 4 and 5. While they do not always fully grasp the more higher level concepts and ideas that we teach and discuss, they benefit immensely just from being surrounded by positive, strong, masculine black men and young black males who have adopted the BPM mindset. The younger boys often understand more than we give them credit for and this is evident in how frequently we hear 5 and 6 year old BPM boys say "I'm going to marry a Black woman and start a Black family." Harmful indoctrination is a long term and repetitive process, empowering re-education must be more long term, intense and repetitive. Our age range now runs from 4 years old to 19 (and will probably be expanding soon).

BPM Grads/BPM For Life

While we had planned on capping our group at boys 17 and under, an unplanned for occurrence began to change that rule by force. Initially, I just wanted to make sure BPM was fun and "cool" enough to keep the boys excited and interested. With that goal in mind I didn't know or realize that so many young black males would find such value and comradery within the group that they would group up, graduate high school, start college and work and still be firmly engrained in the group. This has begun to happen frequently and it is a beautiful thing. I have always been a hawk for spotting and recruiting strong positive brothers to come in as mentors, tutors, volunteers, etc. I had been so focused on finding and bringing in men from around the community that I did not realize we were building and growing the next crop of strong brothers that we would need, from within our own ranks. It caught me off guard when boys that I used to have to pick up and bring to BPM began showing up driving their own vehicles and picking up their BPM brothers as well (a pleasant surprise and less work for me). For this reason we now have young men up to 19 years old and will most likely be expanding further in the near future.

In Addition, due to the fact that our boys have remained in the program into adulthood we had to quickly develop strategies for helping them transition out of childhood (primary school and living with mom) into manhood (going to college or getting a trade, working and being an adult). These requirements caught us off guard a bit due to the fact that we had been so focused on simply ensuring their academic success and keeping them out of the criminal justice system, that we barely thought about the fact that once they achieved success, stayed out of trouble and graduated high school, an entirely new chapter and journey in their lives would begin. Here are a few of the big things that have continued to come up for our high school youth preparing to transition into adulthood;

1. Applying to college and financial aid
2. Preparing for, taking and passing the SAT, ACT or ASVAB
3. Developing an interest in a trade, finding and attending a trade school
4. Finding jobs that they can work while continuing their education
5. Considering entering the US armed forces
6. Getting a driver's license and vehicle

While this list is far from exhaustive, these are some of the things to have in mind when building a long term, enduring program that will take young black males from childhood into manhood.

CHAPTER 4

BPM STRATEGIES AND METHODS

I KNEW FROM THE beginning of BPM that the number one tool in the hand of the oppressor is the mind of the oppressed and that as Dr. Carter G. Woodson said, if you can control a man's thoughts you don't have to worry about his actions. Our young black males in the inner-city have their minds bombarded and attacked EVERY SINGLE DAY with music, television programing and other images that promote nothing positive, Godly or of any value. They inhale, ingest and internalize a thought diet of nothing but filth, materialism, greed, instant gratification, violence, and death. For that reason every strategy and method used in BPM is aimed at impacting the spirits and minds of our boys. The spirit and the mind are closely linked and the constant thoughts that a young man has will begin to shape him at the spiritual level. Here are some of the key methods and activities that we developed and implemented in BPM to destroy the filth built up in the minds of our youth, open their minds to seeking and taking in new knowledge and fill their minds with an ideology that will drive them toward true manhood, dedication to the Black family and rebuilding the Black community.

Lectures and discussions on the true nature of Christ

In BPM we make it a point to teach spiritual principles in a way that our boys can comprehend and apply to themselves, their lives and their current condition. We do not speak in vague, abstract platitudes about right and wrong or good and evil. We teach the history of Christianity and its true foundations in Afrika. We teach our boys to seek a real, intimate relationship with God through their own daily prayers, thoughts and deeds. We teach our boys to see God as Black and to see the God within themselves. We teach our boys that all of your words, thoughts and deeds play a role in bringing you closer to The Most High or moving you further away from him. God is first in the BPM approach because knowledge of and a relationship with The Creator are the first steps toward true knowledge, life and real manhood.

An intense, extensive and unending focus on Real Afrikan/Black History

We have found that of all the tools that exist for reaching and impacting the mindset of Black youth, teaching them their true Afrikan history ranks supreme. In a country where Black inferiority has been taught for hundreds of years and is still taught through the media and Eurocentric education, the most direct and effective way to combat this and wipe out the underlying feelings of racial inadequacy that exist in so many of our children, is to teach them the true track record of accomplishment and achievement of their Black ancestors. This not only corrects the historical record in their minds, it reveals to them what they are inherently capable of today.

For this reason we start every BPM session with a discussion of some issue in our Afrikan history that ties in with current events and that illustrates principles that our youth must learn and follow today. Everything that we teach our youth we teach through the context of or with the backdrop of our Afrikan history. If we want to discuss the importance of education and scholarship, we start with the foundation or example of a great Afrikan scholar like Imhotep or Cheikh Anta Diop. If we want to teach our youth the importance of wealth accumulation or entrepreneurship we look to great Black figures such as Mansa Musa or Madam C.J. Walker. If we want to teach our youth the importance of being able to protect and defend themselves and their families, we start with great Black figures such as Shaka Zulu or Robert F. Williams. This method kills two birds with one stone; it teaches important current information and principles while at the same time providing our youth with factual evidence that retorts and defeats any assertion from anyone that Black Afrikans are or ever have been incapable, incompetent or inferior.

We have a "Black History Sheet" composed of 15 key Black figures that every BPM youth must learn word for word. These figures were chosen because their lives and accomplishments model what we want our youth to aspire to and demonstrate what Black people are capable of in any field of endeavor. Our youth are randomly stopped and quizzed on the historic information that they are required to know; if they demonstrate their knowledge they are rewarded, if it's clear they haven't been studying and staying sharp, they are punished. Real Afrikan history must be a major component in any effort to impact our youth.

Academic Excellence-Competitiveness

One of the most damaging tendencies/habits that I've observed in my ten years of working with Black youth is that many young Black males and their parents will devote years of hard work, dedication and energy to their athletic goals (normally football or basketball), the boys will train, play through injuries, etc. The parents will show up, cheer, travel to watch their kids play and spend $200 on the coolest cleats; but will not bring their sons to free tutoring or show up to parent teacher conferences when their sons are struggling academically. Too many of our youth do not grasp the competitive nature of today's economy and the requirement that flows therefrom to compete even harder in the classroom than they do on the field of play.

For that reason the entire apparatus of the BPM program aims to instill in our boys the desire to compete and dominate in the classroom. Knowledge of self is the first step toward getting our boys to embrace a love for learning. In BPM we use two other tactics to instill the love for learning in our boys, (1) We publicly praise and cheer for our boys based on academic performance but not athletic performance. We purposefully let sports play a secondary, minor role in how we view them and how they view themselves. When a kid makes the honor roll we make sure we stand, clap and acknowledge him with the same fever, emotion, and intensity that he would get if scored a touchdown in the state championship game.

(2) We provide our youth with tutors who personify academic excellence, aid them in understanding their coursework and push them to not settle for average academic performance. I purposefully recruited doctors, lawyers, engineers, small business owners, teachers and other professionals who have advanced degrees so that they can not only tutor our boys in the subject areas of their expertise but also serve as real life examples of Black academic excellence. We strive to create an atmosphere that values education to same extent that our ancestors in Kemet did when producing the greatest scholar in history, Imhotep; and to the same extent that our ancestors in Timbuktu did when knowledge was so valuable that books became a common form of currency for them.

The Impact of The Black Woman in BPM

From the moment that BPM began to experience substantial growth and advancement in organizational structure, even while we were still an all-male youth organization, we made it a point to recruit Black women tutors who were intelligent, credentialed, attractive, and passionate about our people. We did this for 2 main reasons.

First, It is well known that many of the most dynamic and effective teachers in the roughest urban inner city public schools are brilliant Black women. I figured out why this is so by observing my wife at work. Teachers like her bring a combination of strength and discipline along with class and affection into the classroom. They are tough enough to stand firm with the wildest students yet caring enough to do it in a loving way. We observed in our BPM tutoring sessions that women could smoothly teach and handle even the most challenging of our boys, even at times when our male volunteers would become frustrated and want to yell. Our women volunteers simply had a calm grace and patience that our men lacked.

Second, we soon noticed in our efforts to improve our boys' academic performance that while they would put forth effort for us out of respect (sometimes fear), they worked even harder for our women and did not want to disappoint them, although force and fear were not in use. Some of our most challenged and academically behind boys would suddenly be able to solve equations and understand new concepts like never before, once under the tutelage of determined, caring, and attractive, female tutors. There have been times when I would send boys with serious academic issues to be tutored by a female tutor half their size and in the back of my mind be thinking "this boy ain't gone listen." I'd go in during the tutoring session expecting to hear about his insubordination only to be told "he's doing everything he's told and really grasping the information." I would be flabbergasted due to the fact that this same kid would stare blindly at me and stutter when asked a question, when I tutored using respect/fear techniques. I soon figured out what was going on. The boys respected the men and wanted to make us proud, but they had a different type of respect and motivation for not wanting disappoint those beautiful Black women.

Added Benefit

Being around these dynamic, successful, beautiful young Black women also had the added desired impact of destroying the horrendous and damaging stereotypes that many of our boys and men ascribe to concerning our own women. It is not uncommon in Black barbershops around the country to hear Black men throwing around the most outrageous and obscene stereotypes imaginable concerning our own women. The internalization and promotion of these stereotypes by our men along with the media's constant portrayal of lighter women as more beautiful and darker women as less attractive, has left many Black boys feeling the need to pursue only the lightest Black girls or even no Black girls and other races exclusively. I know for a fact that being surrounded by a group of such stunning Black women as we have in BPM has totally shattered those negative stereotypes in the minds of our boys.

Does BPM Only Train Boys?

As BPM grew and people saw the impact it was having on our boys the question constantly came up of when would I expand and work with Black girls. My answer was always short and clear. Never. I was never going to undertake the task of building a girl's' and women's component of BPM, that was a job for a dedicated Black woman and I was unqualified for that job. We have always felt that it takes Black men to teach our boys how to be men and it's the job of women to teach our girls how to be women, many things cannot be taught by a member of the opposite sex. In addition anyone with any bit of experience in this field knows the inherent dangers of impropriety or the appearance thereof in any situation where men are asked to work and interact too frequently with young girls. I was not about to open the door to that in BPM.

In early 2016 a group of dedicated Black women answered the call and organized what is now BPM Girl Power. Now on any given Saturday, in addition to the work we do with our boys, you will see young Black girls being taught knowledge of self, to value themselves, to respect themselves and that they can achieve anything that they put their minds to.

You will see Black women coming together to train the next generation of young Black women who we need so badly to be the wives, mothers, nurturers and feminine balance in our homes, businesses, and other community institutions. The attacks that face our boys are scary, but different yet just as harmful methods are being used against our girls. The women of BPM have taken a strong stance and are preparing our girls to be real Black women.

The activities that our girls partake in our often different and separate from what our boys do. BPM was originally built in a way that promotes and maximizes Black masculinity and clearly we do not want that result for our young girls. The activities specifically tailored to our young girls have included their own educational trips which taught specifically the contributions of our great women ancestors, lectures from brilliant Black female professors, activities which taught them how to properly care for and maintain their natural hair, lessons on cooking, baking, and other activities aimed at instilling the principles of Black womanhood. This component of BPM is growing and advancing fast!

CHAPTER 5

A FEW KEYS IN EMPOWERING BLACK BOYS

Show Them Strength and Love:

WHEN WORKING WITH young Black males it is crucial to establish a relationship based on respect and even a little fear from the start. Most urban Black males have endured rough environments and upbringings which causes them to value toughness and strength. Many of them gravitate toward athletics where their coaches are the only positive Black males they encounter and those coaches normally take a tough no nonsense approach. In addition, young males have a natural proclivity to challenge authority when they see the opportunity. All of these things make it essential that any man seeking to impact these boys (beyond athletics) bring strength and discipline to the table from the start.

Setting a tone of strength and discipline early will pave a smooth road for the next necessity in empowering our young Black males which is showing them love. The fact is that many of the young Black males that I've worked with come in with initial hesitancy and doubt as far as the aims and intentions of the program and volunteers. They often don't understand why someone unrelated to them would be so interested in helping them while receiving nothing in return. Many of them had been hurt, lied to and abandoned by their own fathers making it hard for them to grasp the idea that there were real Black men in the world who would go all out to see them succeed and prosper. The only way to destroy that doubt and skepticism is to show them love and consistency.

Picking the boys up, talking and laughing with them at our meetings, rewarding them when they did good (as opposed to simply punishing them for their bad) and being willing to invest time with them on a consistent basis, are all acts of love that even the most reticent young man finds hard to reject. The key is simply to show them that you care about their wellbeing and a core requirement in demonstrating that to them is **CONSISTENCY**. I knew that BPM would be just another disappointment in these young mens' lives and that the program would ultimately fizzle away, unless I was on the grind fighting for these boys day in and day out over the long haul. I knew that my efforts could not be fly by night, sporadic, hit or miss or "so so" in light of the massive undertaking I had chosen. Children can sense when you don't care and they value structure and consistency. If you're not willing to miss time with your family, rearrange your work schedule and give up much of your hard earned leisure time in order to be consistently present in these kids' lives, STAY OUT OF THIS LINE OF WORK.

Embrace Their Good Before You Target Their Bad

Another valuable lesson that I have learned throughout the years is that you never start with the wrongs and troubles of a teen or pre-teen male immediately upon meeting him. That generally gets things off to a sour start and causes the young man to view the empowerment program as more of a juvenile detention program. That is not the goal. In order for the program to have a real impact, the youth must actually WANT to be a part of it. For this reason, no matter how rude a young man has been to his parents/teachers, etc. and no matter how badly I want to punch him in the chest and let him know he is not as tough as he thinks he is, I always try to start off on a positive note and highlight something that the young brother actually has going for him.

You do not want your program to become viewed by the youth as simply a place to go and be punished. You need them to understand that punishment does not even have to be a part of their experience with the program and that more than anything you are there to help them achieve and reward them when they do. Their negative ways must be addressed, punished and discouraged but there is a time and a place for all things. The initial encounter with a young brother is not the time to jump all over him and beat him down.

It Has To Be Fun

In line with the understanding that the youth must actually want to be a part of the program in order for it to have a maximum impact, you must strive to find ways to make every aspect of the program fun and exciting. Here are a few of the key ways that we accomplish this;

1. Competition: It became clear to me a long time ago that young Black males get 100 percent focused and ready to put forth effort whenever you can turn the task at hand into a competition. When we are teaching Afrikan history or assessing academic progress an easy way to raise the stakes and intensity is to include cash rewards. At the end of every lecture that we do the boys know that there will be review questions with money for those who answer those questions correctly. If the boys are not already motivated to gain knowledge of self from the sheer love for their people's history and heritage, the chance to leave with money in their pockets will serve as an adequate substitute motivation until that true fire is lit.

2. Make It Physical: As I stated above, boys naturally want to be strong and tough and show what they

can do. This is why gangs and violent rap music are so appealing to our boys. Our boys have natural aggression and strength that must be tapped into and properly guided. This is why sparring, wrestling, and weightlifting play such a huge role in BPM. Many young men have come into our program without the ability or skillset to physically defend themselves and subsequently learned a great deal and grew a lot stronger due to the culture and activities that BPM provides. These young men experience a real boost in self-esteem and self-image and they never forget it.

3. The Look: Even the logo designs and colors used in all of our BPM clothing, advertisements and materials were created and designed to convey strength, toughness, and power. These are the traits or attributes that most young Black males want to be associated with whether they find that connection in a street gang, a sports team, or a well-designed youth empowerment program.

4. Compartmentalization: Throughout all of our sessions we are very cognizant of how long we have our young men sitting down in one spot without activity. We are very mindful of the fact that today's youth operate with shorter attention spans and do not cope well with two hour long lectures. For this reason our opening Knowledge of Self lecture is normally

limited to thirty minutes. Our academic tutoring session is limited to an hour and a half and then we move into the physical/athletic portion of the session. Our boys must be taught and retain their history, they must be taught and retain real world life skills, and they must receive intensive help in their core academic subjects. However, all of this must be done with attention to their attention spans.

These are just a few tips to keep in mind so that your program remains interesting and dynamic to the youth and they never get bored with it.

CHAPTER 6

THE BPM GUN CLUB

One of the most controversial, yet attractive, outgrowths of BPM has been our gun club firearm training activities. Personally, I have always been an ardent proponent of Black people defending ourselves and knowing how to do so effectively. That principle played a big part in our choice to include training in boxing and wrestling as core components of our youth empowerment approach. That belief (and urging by my family) also led to my decision to begin purchasing firearms in 2014. As a practicing criminal defense lawyer, I have always dealt with some unsavory individuals and have had to conduct many business transactions in cash. For those reasons it was essential for me to have the tools and skills to protect myself and my family.

Because I knew Blacks have been conditioned to dislike

and fear guns and to associate them with "thugs" and "gangsters" I initially intended to keep my firearms training activities 100 percent separate from BPM. Although I knew that self-defense and defense of family are core components of manhood, I also knew many within the Black community would not be able to grasp that concept and thus there would be some uproar at the idea of young Black males learning to handle firearms. I did not want to fight a battle that was not necessary and I did not want to do anything to detract from the work that BPM was doing.

When I began my own firearms training the only BPM members I included were my younger brother and the adults who believed in exercising their Second Amendment rights. In the back of my mind I always questioned whether Black parents would find my shooting activities too controversial and pull their children out of BPM. While I did receive some backlash from certain sectors within the community, I was pleasantly surprised when the vast majority of my BPM parents expressed their desire for their sons to be taken and trained in the safe and effective use of firearms. Many of the BPM parents had outgrown the common and misguided reluctance within the Black community to be involved with firearms and I soon discovered two equally important reasons for this.

(1) Although I did not realize it, many of the BPM parents had begun to listen to and follow many of my public statements and opinions. Many of the mothers had a latent belief that men should be protectors and for that reason

they supported my position on guns wholeheartedly. Many of their grandfathers had been gun owners and kept multiple guns to protect their families. Seeing a Black man carry on that tradition in modern times was therefore a positive thing in their minds.

(2) Dylan Roof. Prior to the slaughter carried out by this white supremacist terrorist, it was almost impossible for me to convince many Christians of the need for Blacks to protect themselves. Sadly, their view was they would just pray and God would keep them safe from all danger. That view was common in many Black Christian churches and is the result of Blacks being taught a distorted version of Christianity for centuries in America. When this White nationalist went into a Black church and murdered nine unarmed Black parishioners as they prayed, that passivist view went out the window for many Black folk. They then understood they could support being prepared to defend themselves and their families without being labeled as some "crazy militant Black radical."

Many of my BPM volunteers began asking to go out and train with me and many BPM parents began requesting their sons be taught how to safely, responsibly and effectively handle firearms, and in this way the BPM Gun Club was born. I had acquired a number of guns and other BPM volunteers had their own weapons as well. We were given access to private land to train on and so we began enlisting professional firearms and self-defense experts to come out and teach us. As time progressed, "Shooting

Saturdays" became a core part of our movement. To my surprise, shooting never caused us to lose a single child or supporter, but actually gained us many supporters.

CHAPTER 7

FROM AN ORGANIZATION TO A MOVEMENT

THE PROBLEMS AND challenges that our people are faced with are large, multifaceted, and deeply entrenched. Any plan developed to remedy our situation must be as sophisticated, organized and targeted as the efforts that have been utilized to marginalize us. That said, empowering and equipping our youth with the knowledge and tools to succeed despite the obstacles they face is absolutely vital in our push to secure our future. However, youth empowerment is but one front in this battle for liberation. In order to see our people make real gains economically and politically we must organize and fight on all fronts.

We need organizations and institutions aimed at improving our economic position. We need entrepreneurs who will develop innovative products and services and hire our people to manufacture these products and perform those services. We need wealth to back these entrepreneurs and invest in their endeavors. We need to monopolize and control all of the basic businesses that thrive in every Black community; corner stores, hair and nail salons, sea food establishments, daycares, etc. We need political strategists and think tanks to study our condition, foresee future economic and political trends, and prepare us to deal with them. We need our own lobbyists and public interest groups. We need to prepare to self-govern and self-sustain our own communities in every way, from food production and security, to educating our youth, and ensuring their future employment. We need so many things.

One of the greatest benefits that I have observed which flows from recruiting and organizing Black adults to empower and build our youth, is that once you have assembled a group of dedicated individuals with the same mindset, that group can be employed to serve a wide range of purposes on behalf of the Black community. When Black people are given a practical plan and actual daily tasks in carrying out that plan they are much more likely to get involved and stay involved. When they are given real work and tasks to complete they experience the satisfaction that comes from putting in work on behalf of their people and seeing the benefits of that work come to fruition. Once that synergy is created and cultivated around one task (youth empowerment) it can be carried over to other tasks (economic empowerment, political action, etc.). With just five, ten, or fifteen dedicated people a whole community can be changed. A core group of such people can funnel customers to Black businesses or impact the local city council or school board. People who will come out and put in work based on their love for our youth are very likely to be willing to work to improve the Black community in other aspects. By harnessing and directing this energy, a youth program can evolve into an overall community empowerment movement.

CHAPTER 8

DANGEROUS WANNA BE'S

When your faith in God is strong, your purpose is right, your heart and motivations are pure and you pour yourself into empowering our youth and communities YOU WILL HAVE SUCCESS. That is a fact. God will move, the universe will align and the laws of attraction will come into play. Your vision will begin to slowly but surely go from righteous vision to tangible reality. You will attract more like minded people, you will no longer have the carry the load all alone and your impact in your community will multiply. A buzz will grow and more and more people will begin to pay attention and show support. THIS IS WHEN THINGS GET ROUGH.

For the months and years that you labor in the background with few people paying any attention, the level of conflict you encounter from imposters, fakes and wannabes, will be moderate to low, BUT the moment your work begins to manifest, the phonies will come out of the woodwork. There are selfish, greedy, dishonest, conniving, attention seeking hucksters in the Black community whose only real passion is their own fame and success. They want to be known and viewed as committed, dedicated, game changing activists, but they seek that status for all the wrong reasons. Their hearts are not for the youth or the community overall. Their hearts are bent on self-promotion and self-aggrandizement. Because their hearts are not pure, God will not be with them and very few people will gravitate toward their efforts. Unfortunately that will not stop the phonies from attempting to co-opt, feed off, and gain from your efforts. These people will not be around to help you as you work in obscurity, but the moment they see you gaining momentum, reaching the people, and making a larger impact they will run to you like sprinters to the finish line.

Unity is very valuable in our efforts for Black progress and we should not divide ourselves based on minor differences, BUT individuals who truly seek the advancement of our people and nothing else must be careful when dealing with Black people who have ulterior motives. The fact is throughout history our efforts toward freedom and independence have almost always been thwarted by selfish Black people operating on ulterior motives (from Gabriel Prosser and Nat Turner to Huey P. Newton and Fred Hampton of the Black Panther Party for Self-Defense). That being said, as you build an organization that is making a difference and growing consistently, you must also develop methods of weeding out new individuals who show up wanting to "collaborate" or "check out what you got going" all the while trying to hide their true sinister motives. Here are some factors that I consider when evaluating these people;

(1) Their prior body of work on behalf of Black people: What tangible, consistent efforts have they been involved in on behalf of our people and for how long? A person who truly cares about the condition of our people will almost always have a provable track record of working for our people in some way, not just talking about helping our people.

(2) The nature of their body of work: Have their previous efforts been direct and impactful, actually improving the lives of our people or have they been symbolic, simplistic and mainly aimed at gaining attention? A person who truly cares about the condition of our people will work tirelessly for them regardless of whether news cameras are present or not.

(3) Were these people aware of your efforts from the start? And if they were, why didn't they show up until after you had gained steam? These people will often tell you quite frankly "I have been watching you for a while and this thing has really grown." If they were watching you struggle in obscurity why didn't they come and help you then as opposed to waiting until "things had grown?"

(4) Their criminal records: Despite the unfair and corrupt nature of the US criminal justice system, dishonest, shady, opportunistic individuals almost always have legitimate criminal records based on their past dishonest, fraudulent, deceptive acts.

(5) Their intention to takeover or drastically change your organization: These deceitful individuals that I speak of have often tried to initiate efforts of their own and failed miserably due to their improper motives. For this reason they will seek to latch on to successful organizations, not to help those organizations grow, but to attempt to infiltrate, redirect or take over those organizations and use them as vehicles of self-promotion. Be cautious when you encounter "veteran activists" who show up to get involved in your efforts only to immediately begin telling you the number of changes you need to make and different directions that you need to go in.

(6) Always look for REAL PEOPLE: Real people do not have to pretend or audition. They do not have to try to fit in or play a role. They do not have to constantly talk like a politician or car salesman. They can just be themselves confident in the rule that "Real Recognizes Real."

I learned these rules throughout ten years of working on behalf of Black youth and the Black community generally. Clearly there will be other tell-tale signs that a person is not really about what he or she claims to be about when he or she attempts to latch on to your efforts. However, these six guideposts have been very useful to me. You must try your best to keep the snakes out of your yard.

CLOSING

The time for mere talk and endless ideological debate within the so called conscious Black community is over. We do not have time to keep arguing over whether we will call ourselves Hebrew, Moor, Christian, Afrikan, Black or Negro. We have a clear set of problems that we can all see and agree on. It is time for intelligent, dedicated, fearless Black men and women to unite, strategize and get to work building and organizing our people and communities. Our efforts should start locally, be proven, and then expanded. All of our efforts must be practical and targeted. Those who are not about putting in actual work need to be pushed to the margins and ignored. It is time to build.

If you are interested in starting a branch of BPM in your city please feel free to contact me at founder@bpmjax.com.

Made in the USA
Middletown, DE
30 July 2020